BITCOIN

----- ❧❦❧ -----

The Ultimate Beginner Through Advanced Guide on Everything You Need to Know About Investing in Bitcoin, Blockchain, Cryptocurrencies, Ethereum and the Future of Finance

Samuel Rees

© Copyright 2017 by Samuel Rees - All rights reserved.

The follow eBook is reproduced below with the goal of providing information that is as accurate and reliable as possible. Regardless, purchasing this eBook can be seen as consent to the fact that both the publisher and the author of this book are in no way experts on the topics discussed within and that any recommendations or suggestions that are made herein are for entertainment purposes only. Professionals should be consulted as needed prior to undertaking any of the action endorsed herein.

This declaration is deemed fair and valid by both the American Bar Association and the Committee of Publishers Association and is legally binding throughout the United States.

Furthermore, the transmission, duplication or reproduction of any of the following work including specific information will be considered an illegal act irrespective of if it is done electronically or in print. This extends to creating a secondary or tertiary copy of the work or a recorded copy and is only allowed with express written consent from the Publisher. All additional right reserved.

The information in the following pages is broadly considered to be a truthful and accurate account of facts and as such any inattention, use or misuse of the information in question by the reader will render any resulting actions solely under their purview. There are no scenarios in which the publisher or the original author of this work can be in any fashion deemed liable for any hardship or damages that may befall them after undertaking information described herein.

Additionally, the information in the following pages is intended only for informational purposes and should thus be thought of as universal. As befitting its nature, it is presented without assurance regarding its prolonged validity or interim quality. Trademarks that are mentioned are done without written consent and can in no way be considered an endorsement from the trademark holder.

Table of Contents

Introduction 1
    Disclaimer 3

Chapter 1: What Is the Bitcoin? 5
    How the Bitcoin Works 6
    The Value of the Blockchain 7
    The Origin of the Bitcoin 9
    Different From Traditional Currencies 10
    A Protective Option 12
    Designed to Be Limited In Nature 13

Chapter 2: How to Buy, Save and Spend Bitcoins 15
    Get a Wallet First 15
    Buying Bitcoins 17
    Saving Your Bitcoins 20
    Transfer Money In Your Bitcoin Wallet 21
    Where Can You Spend Your Coins At? 21
    Spending In Physical Environments 22
    Public and Private Keys 24
    Using Wallet Addresses 25
    Withdrawing Bitcoins From a Bitcoin ATM 25
    Reviewing a Transaction 26
        Input and Output Differences 28
    Can You Spend Part of a Bitcoin? 29

Chapter 3: Who Runs Bitcoins? 31
Key Rules 32
Can You Technically Own a Bitcoin? 34

Chapter 4: What Gives the Bitcoin Its Value? 35
Government Regulation 37
Media Reports 39
Activities Relating to the Currency 39
Supply and Demand 40
Manipulation 41
Hacking 42
Market Sentiment 43
The Value Cannot Be Inflated 43

Chapter 5: Benefits of the Bitcoin 47
Manage Money Anytime 47
Transactions Can Be As Anonymous As Desired 48
Transparency Ensures You Know Where Transactions Come From 50
Anyone Can Verify a Transaction 51
Fewer Fees 51
Less Likely To Be Impacted By Fraud 52
Growing In Popularity 53

Chapter 6: Disadvantages of the Bitcoin 55
Volatile Value 55
The Coin is Still Developing 56

v

Useful For Questionable Transactions 57

   Restrictions Are Used 58

   Takes a While to Mine 59

   Too Much Power Needed 60

   Is It a Bubble? 60

Chapter 7: How to Invest in the Bitcoin 63

   Contact a Bitcoin Exchange 64

   Order Based on Your Money 65

   Review All Trends 65

   What About Selling? 66

   What About Fees? 66

Chapter 8: Mining Bitcoins 69

   How Does Mining Work? 70

   What Software Works? 71

   Speed Is Important 72

   What Type of Computer Works? 73

   More Computers Are Often Needed 74

   How Much Time Is Needed? 75

   How a Mining Pool Works 76

   What About Cloud Mining? 77

Chapter 9: Trading Bitcoins 79

   Trade On An Exchange 79

   Trade Online Through a Broker 80

   Review Trends 81

Watch the Volume 81

Chapter 10: How You Can Use Bitcoins 83

Transfer Into Fiat Money 83

Move Money Between People 84

Operate Online Banking Services...................................... 84

Chapter 11: A General Look At Other Cryptocurrencies 87

Ethereum 88

Litecoin 88

Zcash 89

Specialized Options 90

More Will Come Later 91

Chapter 12: The Future of the Bitcoin 93

More Countries Start to Use the Bitcoin 93

Brokerage Support 94

More Retailers Start to Use Bitcoins.................................95

More Miners 95

Watch For More Competitors...and a Lack of Knowledge 96

What About a Physical Currency Format?.......................97

Conclusion 99

vii

Introduction

As you look at cryptocurrencies, you will notice that the bitcoin has been relatively popular. Just look at a typical review of the market cap for the bitcoin and you will see just how big it is.

As of the early part of October 2017, the bitcoin has a market cap of $76 billion. This is more than twice the market cap of its nearest competitor in the cryptocurrency world. This is also close to half of the nearly $152 billion total market cap when every cryptocurrency in the world is considered.

It is clear that the bitcoin is one of the most important investments that you could ever utilize. The bitcoin is clearly revolutionizing how money can be handled.

With that in mind, you might have a desire to invest in the bitcoin. This is perfectly understandable as it is a viable cryptocurrency to look forward to. You may also have an interest in using the bitcoin yourself for any intention. Whatever the case is, you should look at what you can get out of the bitcoin if you wish to make it ideal for your life.

You will learn many points about the bitcoin in this guide. It covers aspects relating to how the bitcoin works, how you can buy and spend the coin, what gives the coin its value and how well it can be utilized. You will also see points on how to mine the bitcoin.

Bitcoin

Some other cryptocurrencies are also discussed. But as you will notice, many of them work with the same blockchain pattern that the bitcoin is based around. Of course, the concept of the blockchain system will be highlighted in this guide.

The security of the bitcoin is something to watch for too. This guide has points on what makes the bitcoin easy to apply and use in many situations.

The points you will read about here are important to understand when aiming to get more out of a cryptocurrency. You will be pleased at how well the blockchain system can work for you. More importantly, you will know everything you need to get into the bitcoin investment world.

Disclaimer

Like any other investment, the bitcoin can potentially lose value. There are no guarantees that the bitcoin will be legal in your area either. Additional information on these and other concerns can be found in this guide.

Read through the guide carefully so you have a clear understanding of how the cryptocurrency works. The bitcoin is intriguing but it is just as risky as anything else. You must also be aware of the intricacies of the bitcoin to see what makes it work and also to keep you from being confused or frustrated over how it works.

Chapter 1:

What Is the Bitcoin?

The bitcoin is different from anything you might have seen out there. It works like currency but it has no physical form. It is not operated like any other currency that a national government might issue either. This is very different from what you might expect.

To fully appreciate the bitcoin, it helps to take a look at what makes it special. It is more than just any kind of cryptocurrency. It is the first cryptocurrency to have been made and to become huge in the public sector.

The bitcoin is distinct in that it uses cryptography to keep itself functional. It uses an extensive code system that helps with confirming different transactions.

The key about the bitcoin is that it is a currency that works online and can be used anywhere in the world. It does not go through any intermediaries as it moves from one person to another.

Bitcoin

This is a special currency that is accepted throughout the entire world or at least in spots where it is legal to engage in transactions with it. The coin is very different from what you might see elsewhere so it helps to look at how this is special and distinct.

How the Bitcoin Works

The bitcoin uses a unique standard for keeping it operational:

1. A proper bitcoin wallet must be installed onto a computer or mobile device. Each person who wishes to do business with a bitcoin should have such a program.

2. Proper bitcoins have to be mined so they can exist. Information on mining will be covered later in this guide.

3. A transaction must take place between two parties that have bitcoin wallets.

4. A series of keys must be exchanged between the two people in the transaction. These are the public and private keys.

5. Information on the coin is sent out in the form of a request.

6. The bitcoin community analyzes the bitcoin to make it easy for the transaction to be made. This works through a series of nodes.

7. The information on the transaction will be added onto the blockchain used by the coin. This will come from a new block that goes to the end of the chain.

8. As the transaction is confirmed, the money will go from the initial party to the other.

This is an important process that is vital for ensuring that the currency can work well. This is all about giving the user of the currency extra support for getting a transaction managed right.

The nodes that a transaction goes through include many computers that link to an extensive bitcoin network. The general goal is to make sure the transaction moves through well and is not complicated or hard to follow.

The extensive process only takes a few bits to work. It can take a few minutes for the transaction to be fully confirmed based on how complex it is. But after it is used, it becomes very easy for people to utilize.

The Value of the Blockchain

Many features in the bitcoin make it stand out but it is the blockchain organization that is critical to its success. Thanks to the blockchain system, information on each bitcoin can be provided to anyone.

The blockchain is where the data that goes into a transaction can be read at. It uses an extensive amount of Python programming language but the concepts in each block are easy to understand.

Each block on a blockchain is made with a design that is easy to follow. It lists information on the address that sent the initial coin followed by the recipient address. It does not have to list the name of whoever has taken in the coin although it can do so based on the individual's discretion.

This is followed up by the information on how much the coin is worth in terms of the transactions being managed. The dates for when a coin was made are also listed.

The initial number of the coin or its identifying base is also listed. This refers to the specific coin that was mined. By having each coin contain its own initial number, it becomes easy for a transaction to be listed based on the particular coin or coins being used. As this information is listed, it becomes easier for people to get the most out of the transactions they want to work with.

The Origin of the Bitcoin

Many cryptocurrencies have been produced over the years but none have stuck around as well as the bitcoin. In fact, the bitcoin is the first such major currency of its kind to have been introduced.

The concept of the cryptocurrency was introduced in the late 1990s when the concept of proof-of-work operations could work. This would entail a currency coin being put together through a complex series of equations. This was a unique solution for managing currency although it was not until the introduction of the bitcoin that the currency had actually become viable.

The bitcoin dates back to 2009 when it was first introduced. It was produced as a proof-of-work currency. That is, the currency uses a detailed algorithm and system for confirming the information inside of it.

What happens here is that a coin is mined after a computer solves an extremely complicated equation. The coin is produced after the process is finished and there is confirmation that the coin is real.

Meanwhile, the blockchain will be utilized to produce a strong layout that covers all the information involved in a transaction. This is to ensure a sense of transparency and understanding in the entire process.

The coin would also go through a process where several keys will analyze the code and decipher it within a short period of time. This would assist in producing a currency that can be used in many situations for all sorts of special purposes.

Bitcoin

In 2008, an unknown and anonymous person who goes by the name Satoshi Nakamoto published a paper that discusses how the bitcoin would work. It would be used as a peer-to-peer system for managing cash. A year later, Nakamoto released the first software that would be responsible for producing such coins.

Not much is known about Nakamoto, let alone if someone like him exists or if he is actually multiple people who worked together on the bitcoin. But one thing is for certain in that Nakamoto's developments were extremely detailed. The bitcoin production program was distributed to people through an open source network. The program was made to be easy for the most advanced computers to use as such a computer could work for a while to produce a bitcoin in a proper fashion.

The open source nature of the bitcoin has made it so it can be utilized by anyone. Any person can mine coins provided that one's computer setup is powerful enough for doing so while also having the time and patience for doing so. All bitcoin wallet programs and other applications relating to the coin are made with the same open source standards in mind.

The bitcoin has grown over the years as a peer-to-peer solution that is designed to create transactions that do not rely on trust. It was especially made with the intention of deregulating currency. It was very easy for the coin to develop and become a stronger investment options as people began to notice just what makes it so intriguing.

Different From Traditional Currencies

The problem with traditional government-backed currencies is that they can have their values adjusted rather quickly. Have you traveled from the United States to Canada or vice versa to

Chapter 1: What Is the Bitcoin?

find that your currency was worth a whole lot less in the other country you entered into? Simply put, all currencies have developed their own particular values that make them difficult and in some cases hard to predict. One minute the American dollar is strong against the Canadian dollar, the next minute it is weak.

Of course, some government-backed currencies could be at risk of harm from many factors like economic issues or even corrupt activities. Just think about how the Zimbabwe dollar collapsed a few years ago as it became worthless due to intense inflation.

The bitcoin is much different. It does not come from a government entity. Rather, it comes from everyday people and groups that are capable of mining the currency.

Just look at what make the bitcoin so special:

- It comes from computers that mine the coin, not from the government decreeing that something is produced at a given time.

- It does not have any control from a centralized body. That is, the currency is open to anyone without having to worry about outside factors getting in the way of things.

- The bitcoin does not vary in value by country. The bitcoin comes with the same value everywhere as it can be traded online and transferred into other currencies with ease.

- The process of mining or trading the bitcoin does not have to cost anything extra as the entire bitcoin system is in the public domain. It does cost money to get the materials needed to handle a bitcoin wallet or to start mining coins but those are completely different stories.

A Protective Option

The security of the bitcoin is a critical feature to watch for. There are several good parts of the bitcoin that show just how it will work without any security threats getting in the way of things:

- It is designed to be transparent. It will list details on where it goes and how often people trade with it. The blockchain that lists how it is used can be as long as it has to be.

- Every coin that is mined is unique. Each one comes with its own code and key features that make it special. The coin cannot be easily forged or copied. Each coin can also be tracked by looking up its specific code number that it is identified with.

- Transaction fees involved with this currency are very low. In fact, such fees might not actually occur within a transaction involving the currency.

- People can use many bitcoin addresses for different intentions. Separate addresses may work for different types of business functions for one's record-keeping purposes.

- People can also keep their information anonymous as necessary. The information on one's address will be listed in each transaction but that does not mean the details on where one is located would be included.

Chapter 1: What Is the Bitcoin?

The spectacular world of the bitcoin has become very attractive thanks to these qualities. It is no wonder why so many people have been talking about the bitcoin and how it could be a valuable commerce and investment option for years to come.

Designed to Be Limited In Nature

One very important distinction is that unlike any traditional currency, the bitcoin is limited in nature. This means the coin system is kept under control as people can identify individual coins as they move around the market.

This limited nature also ensures the coin will improve in value over time. It will become more valuable as fewer supplies are made available to the public. This also encourages groups to get towards working on the mining processes for such coins.

The algorithm for producing the bitcoin is limited to where only 21 million bitcoins can be produced during the currency's lifespan.

As of October 2017, there are around 16.6 million coins available on the market.

However, the process for mining such coins has become more complex as fewer of them are available. This means it would take a little longer for coins to be minted. As a result, it may take until around 2110 at the earliest for every single bitcoin in existence to have been fully mined.

The limited number of coins also ensures that it will not be too hard to prepare the mining process. This helps with creating a strong layout for managing money that is not hard to follow. It is a very important currency thanks to how limited it is in its nature.

The bitcoin is indeed a very special type of currency that all investors should look into. Let's look next at how you can get and use bitcoins yourself.

Chapter 2:

How to Buy, Save and Spend Bitcoins

The process of acquiring bitcoins is not as daunting as you might think. You can buy bitcoins and save them for all sorts of special purposes. The places that you can spend your bitcoins at are diverse too.

Note: You do have the option of producing your own bitcoins through a mining process although that would take a good deal of effort and time for doing so. It can still be worthwhile if done right. This point will be discussed later on in this guide.

Get a Wallet First

Before you can use the bitcoin, you must get a wallet. This is a program that goes onto your computer or mobile device. This is needed to help you get the bitcoin to work for you and to ensure you can trade with it.

Bitcoin

All bitcoin transactions require you to have a proper wallet program. Such a program lets you trade the currency with other people. It uses a particular algorithm that will analyze the coins being utilized in the transaction. This helps to produce a fair analysis of what is being traded.

The wallet also reviews the keys that link to your bitcoin account. It analyzes the keys and produces a transaction based on how those keys are to be read. This produces a simple layout that improves upon how quickly the currency can be used.

There are many online wallet programs for you to consider for your bitcoin needs. These include ArcBit, Bitcoin Core, Bither, Electrum, mSIGNA, Bitcoin Knots and Green Address among many others.

There are far too many of these to discuss, what with the bitcoin wallet program being a fully open source option. Fortunately, it does not take much for you to find a wallet when you just look online to see what is out there.

Chapter 2: How to Buy, Save and Spend Bitcoins

The wallet program you download will let you read information on the individual coins you have. It will analyze each point and list details on how well the coins are spent.

You can even use a bitcoin wallet program to adjust identifying information on your transactions for your personal records. You can add private and personal notes to each transaction you make so you can recall what you are doing with the currency. This is a simple feature that improves upon how well you can get a great currency running right.

One quick tip: Look for an open source bitcoin wallet program. The bitcoin wallet code is open to everyone. It only makes sense that you would not have to pay anything to get a wallet ready. Also, just because a company offers a fancy wallet that costs extra to get does not mean that wallet is worthwhile.

Buying Bitcoins

After you have the proper wallet program for getting your bitcoin transactions ready, you will need to buy the proper coins you want.

There are three ways how you can buy bitcoins:

1. **Get onto a proper exchange.**

An exchange is a place that buys and sells bitcoins and other cryptocurrencies. Such a place will list information on how these coins are valued and can let you transfer your coins into other currencies including digital and fiat currencies.

Coinbase is clearly the top option to consider but you have many other options. The choices you have will vary by

Bitcoin

countries as many exchanges only take people who are based out of certain parts of the world.

United States traders can use Gemini and itBit, for instance. Other prominent national exchanges include Coinfloor in the United Kingdom, Bitaccess in Canada and Coincheck in Japan. Even smaller countries have their own exchanges; these include Bits of Gold in Israel and BitBay in Poland.

Take a careful look at any exchange you find though. Make sure the exchange you wish to do business with is legitimate and secure. Look at how you can control your funds through such an exchange too.

2. Go onto a directory that lists details on people who are directly selling bitcoins.

Local Bitcoins and other similar directories offer details on people who are selling bitcoins. These places are useful for how they offer little to no transaction fees. But you should watch for what people might be asking from you when getting coins from such places.

Ask anyone you might do business with about one's experience with the bitcoin. Ask about what that person knows and how that person's wallet is organized. A person who understands how the bitcoin works and has a full program on hand should be easy to trust. Do your research beforehand though so you can be certain you are working with someone who can help you get such a currency ready.

3. Go to a bitcoin ATM.

A bitcoin ATM operates like a traditional automatic teller machine but it gives you the opportunity to buy and sell

Chapter 2: How to Buy, Save and Spend Bitcoins

bitcoins. You can deposit or withdrawal money through such an ATM.

An ATM will print out tickets that relate to the wallet you have. It can look up information on your wallet address and get coins ready. It also uses a strong security protocol to ensure that you are accessing your data and that no one else is trying to break into your wallet.

To make this work, you would need to use a simple process:

- Insert a proper card into the ATM. This could be any kind of banking card. Try and use one that is linked to a bitcoin address or wallet for the best results; this is not required but it is recommended.

- Enter in a bitcoin address for deposit. This should be linked to the bitcoin wallet you have already gotten.

- Insert cash into the ATM.

- Confirm the transaction and the bitcoins will be added into your address.

Bitcoin

Most bitcoin ATMs around the world are found in the United States. This is according to Coin ATM Radar, an online database that lists information on bitcoin ATMs. As of October 2017, the site has around a thousand bitcoin ATMs around the country. There are around 250 such ATMs in Canada and more than 80 in the United Kingdom and 65 in Austria.

With more than 1,600 bitcoin ATMs around the world, it is clear that this option for handling the currency will continue to grow. Check the Coin ATM Radar website to see where such an ATM is located near you.

It might be easier to find such an ATM inside a bank or other financial institution. Do check on what is open where you are so you have a better chance at finding something of value.

In most cases you should be able to acquire as much or as little as you want. You can get a partial coin if you have enough money for it. An entire bitcoin could also be ordered just as well. Considering how much money the bitcoin is worth, you should look at how well you can acquire this currency based on whether you can get just a part of a coin or if you have to get the entire coin in the transaction.

Saving Your Bitcoins

The good thing about saving bitcoins is that you can save them for as long as you want. Many people do this because they know how valuable the bitcoin could potentially become.

The bitcoin is practically being treated like precious metals. However, it is not available in a physical form like with gold or platinum, two other prominent items people like to invest their money in.

Chapter 2: How to Buy, Save and Spend Bitcoins

The value of the bitcoin is relatively volatile but a single coin is still worth thousands of American dollars. People have been very optimistic over the bitcoin in the past few years as people aim to see what makes it stand out and stay valuable as a suitable investment option.

Transfer Money In Your Bitcoin Wallet

Another option you have is to transfer the money in your bitcoin wallet to other people. The process for getting the transaction to work is not too hard. You just need to get the public and private keys for your wallet and the other person's wallet exchanged to get the transaction to move through on the network. It is a simple process that gives you control over how your money is being used in the transaction process.

This is useful if people are asking for money for some reason and need a simple way for getting it transferred. The fact that the bitcoin network is decentralized ensures that the information you need to send will go through quickly. It will only take a few minutes for your money to be transferred regardless of the time of day or week you need help with.

Best of all, this could work even at times when traditional banking services are closed. You could get bitcoins transferred on Sundays, holidays, late at night and so forth. Everything is recorded just about immediately.

Where Can You Spend Your Coins At?

Check around online to see where you can spend your bitcoins at. Various retailers both large and small are accepting bitcoins.

Bitcoin

Most of the places that accept the bitcoin do so online. Overstock.com and Expedia are among two of the more prominent online retailers that accept the bitcoin. The Steam online gaming platform has been taking bitcoin payments too as does the Dish Network satellite television service.

More places are expected to accept the bitcoin as more people start to talk about what the currency has to offer. Check around online regularly to see where you can spend your bitcoins at.

Spending In Physical Environments

Many places around the world have started to take bitcoins for physical payments. That is, they will get access to your bitcoin wallet through a mobile device or card you have.

In most cases you would have to use a mobile device to give a retailer access to your bitcoins. You would have to use a bitcoin wallet app to produce the keys needed for reading your bitcoin account.

The retailer needs to accept a QR code that features your keys. After that code is scanned, the bitcoin transfer process will begin working. This is as all the keys in the transaction are individually reviewed to see what is working in the process.

Chapter 2: How to Buy, Save and Spend Bitcoins

The QR code should be totally unique. It is black and white and features a bunch of squares arranged in a distinct pattern. Every square is perfectly shaped and shaded so it would be impossible to try and forge or produce a fake one. Some QR codes come with larger squares scattered all around to add to the security involved with it. Still, you must keep your QR code clear and easy for a machine to read or else it will not work.

One idea you can use for managing your bitcoins entails using a bitcoin card. Such a card is designed to link to your bitcoin wallet. You could use that card to pay for items with your bitcoins. This would work with a body similar to any other card and would include a simple layout that is easy to handle. You can find such a card from many parties although the BitPay card has become a popular choice. Just be certain that the card you have is utilized at a proper retailer that can actually handle the bitcoin.

Various spots have been accepting bitcoins including some Subway sandwich shops. But you would have to do your research to figure out which places actually take the bitcoin. Not all locations within a chain like Subway have the ability to accept bitcoin payments.

The best thing to do is to visit the CoinMap website at coinmap.org to get information on places that accept bitcoin payments. The site lists more than 10,000 places that accept the bitcoin. Most of these spots are in the United States and Europe although many businesses around the eastern coasts of Brazil and Australia have been taking it in too.

Public and Private Keys

A vital aspect of each bitcoin transaction to see involves the use of public and private keys. Such keys are utilized to allow a bitcoin to be properly spent.

The keys are located inside your bitcoin wallet. These are divided into two parts:

1. Public – This key lists that you own a certain address that can take in bitcoin funds.

2. Private – It uses characters related to your wallet address. It is heavily encrypted and links points on what you are using.

These two keys must be exchanged during a transaction. You and the other person would have to exchange them so all information is listed carefully.

Such keys may be listed on your mobile device or a piece of paper through a QR code. This should be scanned to identify information on your wallet.

Chapter 2: How to Buy, Save and Spend Bitcoins

This only works when you get the proper wallet program ready for your bitcoin use. Check on the wallet you are using so you have more control over the transaction process with the right keys.

Using Wallet Addresses

A great part of using the bitcoin is that you have the option to use as many bitcoin wallet addresses as you want. You can use one wallet address for transactions for business purposes and another for your personal affairs, for instance.

It is free to establish individual addresses for your bitcoin use. But you should still look at how well you can switch from one account to the next. You must also watch for the account your wallet is linked to when paying for something so you can ensure you are only paying for something with the right address in mind.

Be advised that the wallet address you use will be very long. It will include 25 to 34 characters on average. Such an extended length is needed to ensure every address is distinct and cannot be easily duplicated. This is also to support the potential for those to be millions of addresses out there, what with people having the option to use multiple addresses to their names if they see fit.

Withdrawing Bitcoins From a Bitcoin ATM

You already read about how to buy bitcoins through a bitcoin ATM. But how do you withdraw money from your bitcoin account through the same machine?

Bitcoin

To make this work, you need to do the following:

1. Locate a bitcoin ATM that lets you withdraw money from your bitcoin wallet.

2. Load up an application or use a paper wallet that lists details on your public and private keys linked to your wallet.

3. Have the ATM scan those said keys.

4. Enter in details on the money you want to withdraw.

This process uses the keys on your wallet to ensure your identity. This should be used with other security measures in the ATM to ensure that you can get the money you want out of your coins.

It is very easy to buy and spend bitcoins as you get them. Be sure you look at how well these coins can be used so you can get the most out of them no matter what you plan on getting out of this currency.

Also, look at how well you can order bitcoins based on how many you can get at a certain time. You may be allowed to acquire a portion of a bitcoin depending on what you are doing with an ATM. But be certain you have a wallet on hand so you can acquire the coin first.

Reviewing a Transaction

There is one other point to discuss with regards to using bitcoins. As you acquire bitcoins, you will notice a series of transaction details.

Chapter 2: How to Buy, Save and Spend Bitcoins

The specific transaction that you record will be designated by an extensive code with a series of random characters. This is just to record the details on what you have done with your currency.

Several points will be included in the transaction:

- The overall value of the bitcoin transaction

- The input and output for the transaction; this refers to how much bitcoin data was transferred and how much was actually sent to someone

- Any fees that were incorporated in the transaction

- The number of confirmations involved; this would entail many nodes used to confirm that your transaction is legal

- The priority of the trade; this is based on how well that deal was received

- The specific block on the chain for the coin that the deal is listed on

- How long it took for the trade to be fully confirmed; it can take minutes

- The specific time that the deal was made

Several technical scrips will be added as well. These are complex scripts that only a bitcoin wallet can analyze.

Input and Output Differences

The input and output are two things that are noticeable on any transaction. The input refers to the bitcoin address that will be used for sending bitcoins. The output is the bitcoin address for the person who will get the bitcoins.

The output is going to get the coins while the input sends the coins. This is a simple process that is listed on the transaction ledger with particular bitcoin addresses involved. These can be anything so long as proper bitcoin wallets are used on both sides of the transaction.

One thing you might notice when looking at a bitcoin transaction is that there might be a difference between the values of the input and output in the exchange. Bitcoins are only used as records of transactions. Therefore, several exchanges may be linked to one bitcoin address. This might entail one person exchanging money as different transaction records.

Various transaction records may combine to help with facilitating certain exchanges. This means that one person who is sending multiple coins out might only be sending a small amount of a certain transaction to one person. As a result, there would be differences between the input and output numbers listed on the transaction records.

This is a particular point of interest to notice when looking at how an exchange takes place. This is vital for understanding what goes into the transaction you are ordering.

Chapter 2: How to Buy, Save and Spend Bitcoins

Can You Spend Part of a Bitcoin?

A great thing about bitcoins is that you don't have to spend an entire bitcoin during a single transaction. This is great seeing how bitcoins are highly valuable as they are.

A bitcoin is divided into a series of smaller bits known as satoshis. A single satoshi is good for one hundred millionth of a bitcoin.

The smallest possible transaction you can send on a bitcoin network is 5,430 satoshis in size. Therefore, you should be able to use a bitcoin without having to spend the entire thing if you are not interested in doing so.

This is all simple and easy to follow. The process of getting and using a bitcoin is not all that hard to do provided you have the right tools on hand plus a trading partner with the same items.

Chapter 3:

Who Runs Bitcoins?

A great part of the bitcoin is that there are no specific rules as to who can and cannot use bitcoins. People from all corners of the world have bitcoins.

The beauty of the bitcoin is that it is a fully decentralized type of currency. It has not been produced by any governmental entity nor do any countries have a say in how it can be produced or regulated.

The design of the bitcoin is also available to the public. In fact, that design has been utilized to produce other cryptocurrencies, what with the blockchain system used by the bitcoin being such a popular and simple arrangement to use.

No one specifically owns or controls bitcoins. It is up to a community of bitcoin users and investors from all around the world to keep the currency active and functional.

The public domain nature of the bitcoin is critical to see. Since it is in the public domain, it is open for anyone to utilize in various ways. People have the option to create their own software programs for mining coins, transferring them and so forth.

The ability of anyone to use the bitcoin as one sees fit is a big part of what makes the currency stand out. Just look at how well it can operate and you will see how smart it is for your investment needs.

But you must still watch for what you can do when using the coin. A few basic standards should be followed when getting a coin to work for you.

Key Rules

Although there are technically no rules per se when it comes to using the bitcoin, there are a few key considerations that must be utilized. These must be used to comply with the wishes that the founders of the bitcoin had for producing a fully transparent and open currency for the entire public to use. Much of this is with general common sense of in mind but also to create a fair sense of control and support for how the currency is to grow over time.

1. The bitcoin must be fully decentralized.

No individual party, no matter how large or small it is, should have full control over the market. While people have the right to mine and hold as many coins as they want, they should be open with using and offering their coins as they see fit.

People should have the right to hold coins for themselves or to trade them if they wish. The key is that they should have control over their own coins while not interfering with the holds that other people have for their individual coins.

Chapter 3: Who Runs Bitcoins?

2. All blockchain rules must apply when using the currency.

The blockchain rules refer to how the chain is needed for analyzing and listing information on how transactions are run. Although anyone can keep information anonymous if desired, the content in the transaction must be calculated properly. This is to create a detailed layout on the currency.

3. Mining processes must work with software that meets proper standards.

The standards that a software program must use will entail support for solving the equations needed to mine coins. While anyone can develop such a program, the general goal is to create a program that adds a carefully orchestrated security setup that is easy to follow.

4. Everything involved with a bitcoin should be available in the public domain.

The bitcoin is something that is not to be utilized for one's general profit except for when the value of the bitcoin itself increases. Specifically, a person should not try to sell products that involve bitcoin use.

Anyone who wants to sell a bitcoin wallet or mining program should not be charging anything for it. This is thanks to the open source nature of the bitcoin.

Also, the fees that are to be charged for a transaction should be extremely minimal. They must be kept down to allow the bitcoin to be a viable option for transferring money.

Bitcoin

A need to keep such costs down is vital for keeping the currency attractive and useful. It is also to allow people to look into the bitcoin for their own investments.

The profits that people can make off of the bitcoin should be from how the value of the bitcoin evolves. That is, a person can make a profit if that investor buy low and sells high. This profit comes naturally off of the change in the coin's value. It will not come at the expense of any person who wants to use the currency.

These rules are special points that must be followed well. They are general recommendations that encourage people to be careful and to use the cryptocurrency to their best possible efforts.

Can You Technically Own a Bitcoin?

You could hold onto a bitcoin for a while but that does not necessarily mean that you are the true owner of that coin. You simply have the contract to have that particular coin or at least a portion of that coin.

You have the right to hold onto coins for as long as you wish. There are no rules stating that you have to sell off what you have in a certain period of time. This is critical as it ensures you will have the option to keep a coin for as much time as you wish.

The bitcoin is certainly a special type of currency to look for. It is outstanding for being not only easy to use and trade but also simple for anyone to use for many transactions. The fact that it is not owned or regulated by any single person in particular is an especially vital point to explore.

Chapter 4:

What Gives the Bitcoin Its Value?

When you look at your money, you will have noticed that its value has changed over time. It used to be that a bottle of soda could be ordered at a convenience store for a little more than a dollar in the United States. Today that same bottle could be found for closer to two dollars.

Simply put, money always changes in terms of its value. This is the case for any kind of currency. But the bitcoin is a little different.

The bitcoin is like any other currency for how it can change in value at any time. A single bitcoin can be worth thousands of American dollars at a given moment.

But like with any other currency, the bitcoin does have a value that can go up or down. A single bitcoin could be worth hundreds of dollars more or less a week from now than what it is worth right now.

Bitcoin

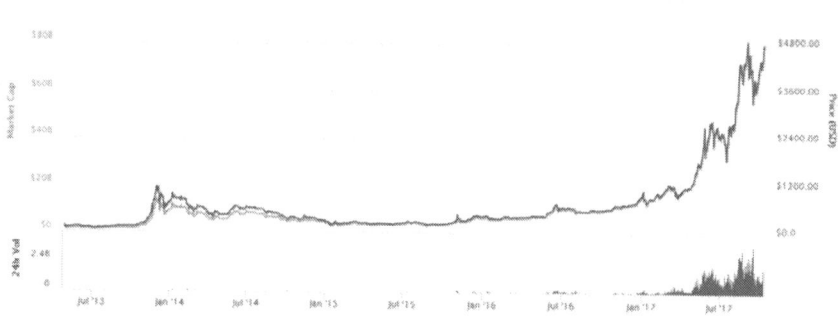

This chart was taken from coinmarketcap.com in early October 2017. It shows the history of the bitcoin's value. Notice how it had been rising in value in late 2013 but stopped and held steady for a while.

But look at how the value of the currency started to grow in 2016. After that, the currency kept on going up and down in spikes. Sometimes it would go up but in other cases it would go down.

That bottom line also shows the volume of the currency. See how in 2017 the volume for trading the currency really picked up big time. This means that the value of the currency could change rather quickly due to so many people trading it.

This historic chart shows just how quickly the bitcoin has risen in popularity in recent time. It also shows that it only takes a minute for the currency to change in value. Sometimes just one move could cause the currency to experience a dramatic spike in its value.

But even with all those changes, the bitcoin is traded just like any other commodity would. You have to look at what gives the bitcoin its value when considering an investment in this currency.

Government Regulation

Various countries all around the world have expressed their own opinions on the bitcoin. Some countries like the United States, United Kingdom and Japan have been rather open to the currency.

But the problem with some countries is that they have been suspicious of how the bitcoin works. The bitcoin has not been allowed in China among other countries around Asia. Specifically, the bitcoin is not recognized as a currency that can be traded even if people who get into the country have bitcoins of their own. The city-state of Singapore has also been monitoring how companies that use the bitcoin do business there but have not actually recognized the bitcoin as a legal currency.

This means that the bitcoin is not necessarily accepted by every place in the world. Any news development where the bitcoin becomes accepted by someone will be very positive. This comes as the bitcoin becomes viable in larger spots.

Bitcoin

Meanwhile, any places that choose to outlaw or at least not recognize the bitcoin will hurt the value of the bitcoin. The decision by China to not accept the bitcoin hurt the growth of the bitcoin for a period of time. This made it harder for the currency to be useful in a large market.

The interest in the bitcoin is still growing as many businesses start to accept bitcoin payments while ATMs devoted to the currency pop up. These places can appear in Singapore and other spots where the government's relationship with the currency is rather frosty.

Watch for any developments that come with the bitcoin based on who accepts them. Any sudden news stories that come about might be a real problem.

Chapter 4: What Gives the Bitcoin Its Value?

Media Reports

The media can make an impact on anything. Whatever the media says will surely be seen as the gospel to some people. This is the case with bitcoins.

The media might add a bunch of reports on things like bitcoin mining activities, companies accepting the bitcoin and new services that make bitcoin usage easier to handle. Such reports from the media could boost the value of the bitcoin.

The media could also keep the bitcoin's value from rising. It might report on new rules that limit how the bitcoin is used. Information on bankruptcies or hacking activities relating to the coin may also hurt the value of the coin.

Even reports on drug transactions and other potentially harmful deals made with the bitcoin could hurt. Anything that happens with the bitcoin in mind could make for a real story in the media's eyes.

Check on news reports relating to the bitcoin regularly to see what is happening with it. Practically any news source will have information on how the bitcoin can be traded. It might be best to look at places like Bloomberg or CNBC or other spots that focus on financial news stories to see what is happening with transactions.

Activities Relating to the Currency

The ways how the bitcoin is being treated are important for understanding how well its value can change. Activities that involve the bitcoin could influence its value.

There are many points that could cause the bitcoin's value to increase:

- Increased mining activities make it easier for people to find bitcoins, thus making them more available. The fact that fewer coins are available for mining also makes the value go up.

- Companies accepting the bitcoin also make it valuable as the bitcoin can go further in more spots.

- The added functionality features of the bitcoin could be a factor. These include factors like the bitcoin being available in a card form for spending in many spots.

There are also some activities that could keep the value down:

- A slowdown in mining suggests that the currency might not be in as much demand as people would wish.

- Problems relating to the bitcoin network, particularly hacks or downtime on any major servers, could keep the bitcoin from being helpful.

- The impact of other cryptocurrencies could hurt as well. Sometimes competing currencies might steal the bitcoin's thunder for a brief bit of time.

Supply and Demand

The concept of supply and demand is easy to understand. When the supplies are limited, the price of something becomes high. Meanwhile, the demand for a product might trigger the production of a larger supply of something; even then the

Chapter 4: What Gives the Bitcoin Its Value?

value of that item might go down depending on what happens with it.

The bitcoin will certainly have its value impacted by supply and demand. While there are millions of coins out there, some of them might not be accessible as people may be holding onto them for a while. This keeps those coins from actually being available, thus reducing the amount that is out there.

In addition, mining activities will only emphasize how the supplies for the currency are limited. After all, there are only a certain number of coins available for use.

The price of the bitcoin may rise as supplies become limited. As fewer coins are available for mining, the demand will start to increase as people want to find coins for their own. This in turn may cause the value of the coin to increase as the supply starts to dwindle.

This is actually the main consideration that some people use when trying to create their own new currencies through initial coin offerings. They believe that by limiting the total number of coins that can be produced, it becomes easier for those coins to be valuable as the demand gets higher. With people willing to pay more for something that is finite in nature, it might be easy for people to get more out of the coin investments they get themselves into.

Manipulation

Any investment out there could be manipulated. Just look at penny stocks and you will see what this means. It only takes one massive trade of a small penny stock that hardly ever gets traded to directly influence its value. This comes as the volume for trading suddenly experiences a dramatic short-term increase as the value of something either goes up or down.

The bitcoin is just as vulnerable to market manipulation as anything else. In this case, a single investor might buy a large amount of coins on the open market. This would cause the value of the coin to increase.

But shortly after that, the investor would sell off those coins. This comes as the investor would have made a profit on the deal.

This would require an extensive amount of effort for an investor to complete, what with the bitcoin being worth so much money as it is. But the threat of market manipulation is real and cannot be ignored.

Even with this in mind, it is not necessarily illegal for people to alter the market in some way. The fact is that anyone can trade these coins so long as they have enough to work with at a given time.

The worst part is that most people who manipulate the market might not be aware that this is what they are doing. They might not notice that the trading volume for a currency is not as strong as it might usually be. This in turn causes the currency to change in value rather quickly.

Hacking

Although the bitcoin system is very strong and complex, it is still at risk of hacks. There is always the potential for a hacker to get into a bitcoin setup to break into the code used for it. This could cause some codes or other bits of data relating to the bitcoin being released to the public.

Chapter 4: What Gives the Bitcoin Its Value?

Any breaches or other threats could be a significant problem. The bitcoin system is organized to where it must be regulated well and protected with enough security features. Although the security of the bitcoin is strong thanks to the extensive amount of work needed for mining a coin, there is always going to be some kind of security risk involved with the bitcoin. Be aware of this as any hacks or breaks into the system could cause the value of the coin to decline dramatically.

Market Sentiment

Like with other investments out there, the market sentiment will play a role in how the bitcoin trades. There is always a potential for the bitcoin to go up or down in value based on factors like what people are thinking about the coin in terms of how people are accepting it or how it would compare with other currencies. The developments of the coin could also make an impact.

It is tough to figure out how market sentiment works. The general public operates in many ways. Some like to be very technical when analyzing how the bitcoin changes in value while others just look at what is happening around it.

Whatever the case might be, the market sentiment involved with the bitcoin will play a huge role in how its value may change. Be aware of this as you are looking to invest in this currency.

The Value Cannot Be Inflated

The factors that influence the bitcoin's value are great but there is one point that can certainly be ruled out. The bitcoin is not a currency that can be inflated in terms of its value.

Bitcoin

Government-issued money can be inflated by the government as it sees fit. This could come from limiting how it is produced or expanding its production. It could also come from government control over the economy or even how the currency is organized.

Inflation is often utilized to try and catch up with other countries or to make it easier for governments to raise funds. But in reality, inflation often makes it harder for people to use their money. Unless they get interest on their investments or they get pay raises on a regular basis, it becomes harder for people to actually use their money. What was worth something good at one point now becomes harder to utilize. Your dollar will not be worth as much years from now as it is today.

This is where the bitcoin comes into play. You will see that the bitcoin can grow in power and will stay at around the same general value regardless of how bad inflation gets to be.

The bitcoin is not at risk of problems relating to the inflation. In fact, its value practically changes based on how other currencies might be inflated. As other currencies start to become weak, the bitcoin begins to appear as a more viable investment object. This is thanks to the lack of centralization on the bitcoin's part.

The community that surrounds the bitcoin focuses more on how well the currency can grow than it does over how to make money. Besides, when the currency grows in prominence and functionality, the bitcoin will already become more valuable. It is through hard work and effort and not through inflationary actions that the bitcoin becomes a more viable and profitable endeavor for anyone to enter into.

Chapter 4: What Gives the Bitcoin Its Value?

That valuable point makes the total cost of the bitcoin rise. It practically keeps itself from being weak in a world where inflation is prominent all the way through.

Look carefully at how well the value of the bitcoin can change over time. There is always the chance that the value of this currency can change in many forms. Be aware of what can be used when finding such a great currency for your use.

Chapter 5:

Benefits of the Bitcoin

The bitcoin continues to grow in popularity as more people are starting to see how well it can be used for many transactions. But as people start to notice over time, the bitcoin is more intriguing in its functionality than what many might expect.

The bitcoin is a very attractive cryptocurrency thanks to many factors. Let us take a look at a few of these important points that show how special the currency truly is.

Manage Money Anytime

The bitcoin gives you the ability to send and receive money from any place at any time that you want to get it out at. The strong versatility of the bitcoin provides you with an option for payment purposes that fits perfectly with the needs you hold.

The bitcoin works just like any other payment option in that you can get your money spent in any way you see fit. This is a special feature that gives you something extra for managing money.

More importantly, the currency can work at any time that you see fit. The open nature of the currency ensures that you can

Bitcoin

get your money managed at any moment without having to wait far too long to make it functional. This is an advantage that adds to how well the currency can be used for any intention you have.

Transactions Can Be As Anonymous As Desired

One part of the bitcoin that many people like is that the transactions involving the currency can be made as anonymous as one wants them to be. But this is not necessarily the "anonymous" you think it might be.

It is true that a bitcoin transaction can be handled with transparency in mind. But anonymity is possible thanks to three points:

1. You can use a bitcoin address that is not tied to your identity.

The bitcoin address you use does not have to be linked to your identity based on its protocol. That is, you can create a totally new bitcoin address at your liking as you see fit. Your private key can be prepared in any way. There is no need to submit your personal information to anyone, thus ensuring your identity is secure.

As mentioned earlier, you do have the right to use as many of these bitcoin addresses as you wish. Just be certain that you keep tabs on how all of them are organized. This is to keep you from using the wrong address at the worst possible time.

2. **All transactions involving a bitcoin are not tied to a user's identity.**

You can transfer the bitcoin to another address without sharing your personal information at all. You will have the full right to send it off to someone else based on what you want to spend it on and so forth.

3. **Transaction data is sent through random nodes on a peer-to-peer network.**

IP addresses are used to get bitcoin nodes to link to one another. But the nodes used for transferring information will be random based on what is available within the bitcoin network. Therefore, your IP address will more than likely not be exposed.

The bitcoin community will confirm transactions and see that all keys being used are accurate. The community does not necessarily have to notice any personal bits of data. It just needs to see that the records for which wallet addresses have acquired particular coins match up with one another. It is about keeping the information easy to confirmed.

In short, your information is not going to be easily exposed in the bitcoin transaction process. You will keep your data and information safe without being at risk of having anything lost in the process.

Transparency Ensures You Know Where Transactions Come From

While the information that you send out can be anonymous, details on where a transaction is going to and coming from will still be made available. The bitcoin has a public ledger of every transaction that takes place with it.

When you look at the blockchain information on a single bitcoin, you will learn points on:

- When the coin was introduced on the market

- How many times it has been transferred

- The addresses that handled the currency

- Any identifying bits of information that either side wishes to share if applicable

While the information can still remain anonymous as desired, the fact that the bitcoin is transparent is a critical point to see. You will see how the currency is being used and that it is being handled in a careful manner.

This is a dramatic difference from what you might see out of traditional physical currency. The problem with physical currency is that it can be moved to any place without anyone knowing what it had been used for. For all you know, the physical money you have right now could have come from a bank heist. Maybe it might have been used in a drug transaction.

With the bitcoin, you at least know where your currency is going. You can look up information on what it has been used for as you see fit.

Of course, there is still the concern that your bitcoin could have been used for potentially dangerous actions. This is something that will be discussed in the section of this guide dedicated to drawbacks of the bitcoin. The lack of a physical body at least ensures that your currency will not have experienced fatigue or possible damage during illegal activities. Don't forget that the currency will more than likely not have been infringed upon or copied.

Anyone Can Verify a Transaction

The peer-to-peer setup of the bitcoin is designed to allow people to confirm their transactions well. After the information on a transaction is sent out to a network, bitcoin miners will verify that move. The added information is placed in a transaction block and eventually solved in a matter of minutes. This confirms the movement of the coin.

It can take around ten minutes for a transaction to go through though. This is due to the need to mine a new block on a chain.

Fortunately, you will not have to wait to get your item or service if you are using your bitcoin for a low-cost transaction. Some retailers might make you wait a bit if the transaction is high in value though. They don't want to be victims of fraud.

Fewer Fees

This next advantage is great for buyers and retailers alike. The fees involved are extremely minimal.

Bitcoin

In most cases the fee for a bitcoin transaction would be worth 0.00000001 BTC. If the bitcoin were around $4,500 in value then that means the transaction would have a fee of $0.000045.

In short, the total fee that comes with a bitcoin transaction would be extremely small. You might not even have to pay a fee at all.

Individual retailers do have the option to charge whatever fees they want. But considering the simplicity of the system, any cases where a noticeable amount of money would be charged would be very slight. It might be less than a dollar in value.

This is great for buyers but it is even better for retailers. The problem with managing traditional debit or credit card payments is that a retailer would have to spend a certain fee on handling such a transaction. This might be good for 2 to 3 percent of the value of the entire deal. This often forces retailers to increase the prices for their goods just to cover the transaction fees.

With bitcoin payments, such high fees are a thing of the past. The retailer does not have to waste money or time on getting such fees managed.

Less Likely To Be Impacted By Fraud

The bitcoin is an extremely complex instrument that takes a while for it to be mined. The code used to prepare it and make the coin useful is extensive and complex, thus making it hard for anyone to try and duplicate. It is with this in mind that the currency is fully protected and secured.

Chapter 5: Benefits of the Bitcoin

The bitcoin is not as likely to be copied as with other currencies. This keeps forgery or fraud from taking place.

Counterfeiting is prevented by the bitcoin network having to ensure addresses for coins are valid and have the right values attached to them. The detailed ledgers on each coin keeps such data secure, thus preventing fraud from occurring.

This is vital when the value of the bitcoin is considered. Having a digital currency on your hand is always helpful as it keeps you from potentially losing something important.

Even with this, you should still look at how the bitcoin data you have is kept. You would need to keep a secure tally of your records for acquiring the bitcoin to ensure that you have proof of your data as you see fit. The complex nature of the bitcoin keeps you from having to spend far too much on the coin at a time but it is still worth noticing.

Growing In Popularity

As you read earlier, the bitcoin has been growing in popularity. It has been accepted by more people over a larger network and is being included in many trading activities.

More people are accepting the bitcoin for transactions and other activities. The bitcoin is also being incorporated as an option for managing money in parts of the world where traditional currency functions are not easy to use or support.

There is still a sense of concern over which countries are likely to accept the currency down the line. Plenty of effort is needed to allow the currency to become more valuable and useful as time goes along.

Bitcoin

As the bitcoin keeps growing in prominence, it becomes clear that it is something everyone will want to watch for. You will need to see what makes the bitcoin stand out and make it useful if you are looking for an ideal investment opportunity.

Chapter 6:

Disadvantages of the Bitcoin

Although the bitcoin is a very special and useful type of cryptocurrency that is worthy of your time, it is not in any way a perfect investment option. There are plenty of negative aspects of the bitcoin that deserve to be explored just like with anything else you might want to invest in.

Volatile Value

The bitcoin is a currency that is extremely volatile in its value. Because it can get to be worth loads of money, there is always the potential for the currency to change in value.

Look at a typical price chart for the bitcoin and you will see how quickly the value of the coin can change. It could go up or down by hundreds of dollars at a given week.

Refer specifically to the price history chart you saw earlier in this guide. You might have noticed that as the currency became more popular over time and was traded more often, the value started to change dramatically. It kept going up but there were often times when the currency's value dropped down sharply.

The bitcoin is something that requires a bit of extensive analysis before you choose to invest in it. You have to invest carefully based on the trending nature of the currency. It might be going up at a time but there are many variables that could make it go down just as well.

If anything, the bitcoin could be a more appealing long term investment when the potential for growth is considered. That does not mean the growth of the bitcoin will last forever or is even guaranteed. All investments have their breaking points and could start to lose value after a while. You must watch for this if you wish to get something special out of an investment like this.

Naturally, you could get a huge gain on the value of your bitcoin. But be careful as there is just as much of a risk of the bitcoin to fall in value as it is for it to grow.

The Coin is Still Developing

Although the bitcoin is a popular currency option, it is still developing. It is not necessarily perfect as there are still chances for the currency to be broken into.

The security features of the bitcoin are constantly being updated as a means of ensuring the coin will be less likely to be hacked into. There are also developing going on in terms of trying to make the bitcoin easier to process without spending too much time in the process.

The coin is not going to be stronger overnight. It is vital to see how well the currency is going to grow and thrive after a while.

Useful For Questionable Transactions

Although the bitcoin is transparent, it can still be anonymous in terms of how its transactions are managed. That is, people can keep from having to post information on whom they are within the individual transaction notes they are producing.

This means that the bitcoin could be used for managing many questionable or potentially harmful kinds of transactions. In particular:

- Money laundering activities can take place with bitcoins. This is where money that is illegally obtained is fully covered up. In particular, the currency would become expensive.

- Drug trades could take place with bitcoins. People can use bitcoins to get funds for illegal rugs moved around without worrying about the money being too easy to track down.

- Terror-related activities could also be funded with bitcoins. The ability of the bitcoin to move through any account with a bitcoin wallet makes it so the currency could go between people involved with terror organizations.

- Adult-oriented transactions could also take place with bitcoins. These transactions include the sale of pornographic materials.

The bitcoin is something that can be used for many of these unusual transactions that might be suspicious to some. This can be a real problem as there is no way how people could tell if their bitcoins have been used by certain people who engage in these difficult activities.

Fortunately, you are not going to be at risk of people coming into your home and inspecting anything or seizing your money if you have acquired a bitcoin that was used in some kind of illegal transaction. The fact that such transactions are hard to trace ensures that this will not happen.

But the fact that such harmful transactions can take place with the bitcoin in mind makes it so there is no telling what can happen. There is always a potential for the bitcoin to possibly be subject to further monitoring and analysis based on what happens with it in the future.

Restrictions Are Used

Not all places around the world are accepting the bitcoin. Some countries have placed extreme restrictions on how the bitcoin can be used and what people can do with their currencies.

Most places that refuse to use bitcoins are spots that are overly suspicious about how well these coins may work. Many feel as though these coins could be difficult to handle and might be potentially dangerous in some form.

Among the countries that have outlawed the bitcoin including Bolivia, Ecuador, Bangladesh and Kyrgyzstan. They have frowned upon many aspects of the bitcoin, most notably its support for anonymity. Bangladesh in particular outlaws the bitcoin as it goes against the extremely strong anti-money laundering policies used in that country.

Chapter 6: Disadvantages of the Bitcoin

Many other parts of the world have been suspicious as to how the bitcoin works too. China has not been trading the bitcoin and has not allowed retailers or other groups around that country to trade the bitcoin. Meanwhile, the Singapore government has not officially certified the bitcoin as a legal currency although it has been monitored in terms of how businesses use it.

There is always a chance for countries to be more open to the currency as time goes by. But until then, it is difficult to figure out just who could potentially work with the currency and how it can be utilized in some way.

Takes a While to Mine

You will learn not long from now in this guide about how the mining process for creating bitcoins works. It is a useful process that is easy to handle but at the same time it can take a while for the bitcoin to be mined properly.

The difficulty surrounding working with an equation that has to be solved for getting a bitcoin produced is immense. You might have to spend months or years to mine a bitcoin depending on the complexity of the situation and the computer you have. The fact that fewer coins are coming about will only make it harder for certain currencies to be mined just as well.

Of course, you can always join a mining pool to make it easier for you to get a coin produced. Still, you would only get a certain amount of that coin based on the power you put into the process. Seeing how popular the mining process is in general, you might not get all that much out of the coin through a pool unless you are really devoted to it and have invested in quite a powerful setup.

Too Much Power Needed

What is also concerning is that the mining process requires a massive amount of power on your end for producing a coin. A stronger computer would be required for mining a coin as well as possible. It would require a consistent amount of power and a very strong graphics card. You would also have to keep the entire space cool as the computer could easily overheat.

Besides, it would be a waste of time to use your current computer to mine bitcoins. As you will see in the chapter all about mining, the computing power needed for getting a coin mined would be significant. It would definitely be well outside the general needs you hold.

The worst part is that sometimes a computer that mines the currency could break down. The immense power requires can cause a computer to overheat. This in turn could make it break down. This not only stops the mining process but also requires you to buy a totally new mining setup just to make it work again.

The cost associated with powering up a computer for mining purposes could be prohibitive too. The added energy could add up on your electric bill in your home or office. This would be even more difficult to manage if you have lots of computers connected at a given time.

Is It a Bubble?

One of the most common concerns people have about something is that it might be a part of a bubble. This means that something will increase in value and then collapse and fall apart quickly.

Chapter 6: Disadvantages of the Bitcoin

This is a problem that happened with websites in the late 1990s and with the housing market in the 2000s. The demand for certain things kept rising and their values were climbing. But suddenly for a variety of reasons, the market bubble burst and the values collapsed, thus causing many people to lose their money on their investments.

Considering how so many bubbles have happened for many investments in the past, it is understandable as to why so many people would be worried about the bitcoin. They are often afraid that it is part of a bubble and that its value will also decline.

The arguments that suggest a bubble could burst are as strong as those saying that the bitcoin is a legitimate option for investment use.

We need to look at a few points relating to how the currency is run:

1. The bitcoin has already gotten its fair share of competitors on the market. These include many smaller currencies aiming to steal its thunder.

2. The currency has been carefully developed and is in the public domain so it is not going to easily be harmed in some way.

3. The overall acceptance of the currency has been growing.

4. Even with all these factors, the bitcoin is still something many countries around the world are suspicious about.

5. Digital technology is often tough to predict or come by.

6. There is always the chance that something new will come about and become the hottest new investment, thus causing people to leave the bitcoin behind.

The pros and cons of the bitcoin are clearly visible. The pros suggest that it will last for a while but the cons say it might collapse in a bubble. Whatever the case is, this is certainly an investment that anyone who is interested in it will have to watch for in terms of how it can grow.

Be aware of all these issues that come with the bitcoin when it comes to using it for investment purposes. Watch for what you can get out of the coin and make sure you are aware of how well it can be used in any situation.

Chapter 7:

How to Invest in the Bitcoin

The bitcoin is a very special currency in that you can invest in it right now. While many people like to invest in different currency pairs on the forex market, you have the option to simply invest in the bitcoin as it is.

Of course, the value of the bitcoin is typically compared with that of the American dollar. Then again, the same can be seen with any other commodity out there.

In fact, the bitcoin is traded just like any other commodity on the market. The big difference is that you could get a bitcoin to hold for your own for as long as desired. This is different from other commodities where you would have a contract to trade something like a few barrels of oil or whatever else is out there.

Your ability to invest in the bitcoin is important to your success in handling it well. This chapter is all about the things you should do when investing in the bitcoin.

Contact a Bitcoin Exchange

Because it is a rather new investment option, you are not necessarily going to see people on Wall Street or some other high-end financial center trading the bitcoin. You probably won't even find information on its value in your local newspaper.

You would have to go online to get details on what is available for your investment use. Considering how the bitcoin is always open for trading, this may be for your benefit.

With all this in mind, you would have to go online to invest in the bitcoin. The places you can choose from for investing are diverse but it helps to at least see what is open.

To start, you have to contact a bitcoin exchange to get details on what is available for your investment needs. Naturally, you can find many major sites like Coinbase or Kraken or Cex.io out there for your trading desires.

But when finding such places for trading, you have to watch for what is available. Look at the sites that are available based on their features, the currencies available and any other key technical points they have. Look and see if they have useful analytical features to help you understand what is going on with the bitcoin.

Chapter 7: How to Invest in the Bitcoin

Order Based on Your Money

You should have the right to order bitcoins based on the specific amount of money you have. In particular, you should be able to order only a small amount of a coin if you do not have enough money to buy a full coin.

Seeing how the bitcoin is worth thousands of dollars, a bitcoin exchange should give you access to smaller amounts of the currency as you see fit. Check on the terms that a site offers so you can get an order ready well enough.

Review All Trends

As you look at the bitcoin, you have to see how it is being traded. The bitcoin should be treated like any other investment or commodity. It has its ups and downs like anything else you could look for.

See how the coin is moving up and down based on trading volume and any developments involved. Look at how market sentiments might develop based on the ups and downs that are on a chart.

You can use as many analytical points on the bitcoin as you wish. Talking with an investment firm that supports the bitcoin and other similar currencies is always good to do although the information they offer is just one bit of advice you could use.

Whatever it is you do, you must think about how well the bitcoin moves and that you are careful with it. Remember that the bitcoin could still lose value at any moment. Keep tabs on everything happening with the bitcoin so you know when its value might drop or build up plus what could be causing such changes to come along.

What About Selling?

You should be able to sell the bitcoin at any time on an exchange. The protocol should be similar to what you used when buying the coin. You would have to provide your wallet address to make it work well.

The specific value that you sell your bitcoin at must be reviewed well. You should be able to get the bitcoin sold at a value that is based on when you triggered the sale action. Although it does take a few minutes for you to get the bitcoin transaction to be finalized, you should have the value of your bitcoin reserved based on the specific time when you deposited something.

This is important as the value of the bitcoin can change dramatically in just a bit of time. It could change by several dollars in a minute's time. Getting the trade to go at the exact time you want it to work at is important to see. An exchange should give you the support you deserve for managing the coin.

What About Fees?

As mentioned many times already, you should not have to bear with too many fees. But do be aware that many exchanges will add fees to their transactions to make it easier for them to work. These fees will be very minimal though as they should be less than half a percentage point of your transaction's value at the most. Remember, the bitcoin is organized to where it does not require extensive costs for managing it.

Chapter 7: How to Invest in the Bitcoin

The fees should be listed by whoever you are doing business with. Do not stick with anyone who is secretive or not willing to be direct with you on the fees involved with a transaction.

Make sure the fees are not too high either. You do not want to spend more on your fees than what you can afford to handle.

You need to do business with someone who understands your needs and will help you with managing any kind of transaction of value to you. This means that person should be willing to tell you any fees that are involved without surprising you.

Investing in the bitcoin is simple and easy to do. Look around online to see who will offer you great bitcoin investment solutions and you will see just how easy it is for you to get more out of the bitcoin.

Chapter 8:

Mining Bitcoins

It is always useful to but bitcoins on an exchange. But wouldn't you rather get them for free?

You can do that if you mine your own bitcoins. The mining process produces the coins that anyone can use.

But the mining process requires an extensive amount of work on your part. It also requires a sizeable investment. You do have the option to get into a mining pool but that would not necessarily give you far too much of a return on what you have.

Mining bitcoins sounds appealing and can help you get free coins for your own use. But you must be aware of the realistic concerns that come with mining those coins.

When you read about people mining coins, you are not getting the full story. Places that mine these coins are often larger entities that can handle loads of computers in their own dedicated rooms with their specific generators and other power-related features. Such spots are extremely intricate in nature.

Be advised that the process for getting a bitcoin mined could be tough to complete. This is not always easy to do but it can be useful if you look at how well the mining process is run.

Bitcoin

How Does Mining Work?

To start mining, you need a computer and a software program. These go together to help you generate the data needed for producing a bitcoin.

The process for mining bitcoins entails a number of critical steps:

1. A computer will use a processing program that analyzes different codes and equations. The program will need to solve these equations.

2. The computer will analyze the parts of each equation and spend time solving every one. The equations are very complicated and can take a while to finish off. The equations also vary based on the specific coin being produced; they become more complex as fewer coins are made available.

Chapter 8: Mining Bitcoins

3. As the information is confirmed, a block is produced. This includes information on the bitcoin.

4. Multiple blocks must be created to establish a full blockchain. This will create all the information for the bitcoin.

5. After the information is gathered and resolved, a bitcoin is produced.

This mining process works as a proof-of-work setup. A computer that can solve certain equations will have to complete those tasks to get a coin ready and open for use.

What Software Works?

You can find many bitcoin software mining options on the market today. These are free to use in most cases, what with the bitcoin system being open to the public.

The programs that are available are amazingly diverse. Choose from options like Bitcoin Miner, BTCMiner, CGMiner, RPC Miner and much more. These work on most major operating systems.

Such programs can vary based on what they offer. Look for features like the following:

- How it triggers mining activities

- Programming features that lists technical information on the mining process

- Speed control features

- Real time updates; these include points on the speed of your miner, your hashrate, the fan speed and the temperature of your computing unit

- Fan control support; this keeps the computer from overheating while mining

- The ability to identify new blocks in a chain quickly

- Support for many processing units

- The ability to link your bitcoin wallet to several processing units; you would have to register each computer that uses a program for this to work

Again, be certain that the bitcoin wallet you are using is free and easy to utilize.

Speed Is Important

A critical thing to see in the mining process entails the speed of a computer's mining options. The mining process is measured based on the number of hashes produced in one second. When more hashes are involved, it means the computer can produce more computations in a single second. This reduces the amount of time needed for the computer to produce a coin.

Some of the more powerful mining rigs out there can work with 1 TH/s speeds. This means it can handle one terahash per second or one trillion hashes.

The stronger the computer, it faster it can work. Be aware of this when planning your mining activities.

Chapter 8: Mining Bitcoins

What Type of Computer Works?

A strong computer is needed for the bitcoin mining process to work. It must be able to review all equations well and get enough blocks prepared after a while.

There are several things that have to be seen in a mining computer:

- A computer needs a processor that can handle more data at a time.

- Plenty of memory is also required in the mining process. At least 16 GB of RAM is needed to allow the computer to identify more equations at a time.

- A strong video card with 8 GB of memory or more is also needed. This adds to how well the computer can analyze data and visualize what it is processing.

- A large disk drive is also required. A single bitcoin chain could be 100 GB or more in size.

- A strong power source must be used. Anything that can link to a generator to keep the mining process going at all times is always worthwhile.

- A cooling system is also vital. The immense power needed to mine a coin can cause a computer to become hot. A strong fan system or coolant material may be used. The computer must also be vented well so the heat generated does not stick around for long.

- An extremely fast online connection is also needed. Something that can handle 500 Mbps download speeds or greater is vital. A modem that can handle those speeds is needed too.

The computer must be strong enough to keep working without delays. Look at how well the computer you plan on using can be organized so you can get it all running fast.

Even more importantly, be certain you can actually afford such a computer. You would have to pay at least $3,000 to get a computer just for mining purposes.

Don't forget about the extra costs associated with keeping it running; the energy generated may be high. The cost for a very strong online connection could add up each month too.

The bitcoin might be worth a good deal but so is the computer needed for mining it. Even with that in mind, it would still take a while to actually mine something.

More Computers Are Often Needed

The biggest problem with just trying to mine bitcoins is that it would take forever to complete the process. Just one computer is not necessarily going to work.

You might need to get several computers linked up to one another. You could have two or more mining computers connected online and linked to the same bitcoin address that you want the profits to go to. With two computers, you would get your bitcoins ready in half the time. But you would still have to spend lots of money just to get those two computers ready.

Chapter 8: Mining Bitcoins

This is a key part of why so many people who mine bitcoins are part of larger businesses that can afford the cost associated with getting many computers linked to the same account. They are groups that can get bitcoins and then sell them off to others for a profit.

A business with lots of computers would have to get multiple bitcoins to cover the cost associated with starting up an immense mining operation. Seeing how it takes less time for a company to get all of these items mined properly, this is clearly for its own benefit.

How Much Time Is Needed?

Be prepared to spend an extensive amount of time mining a bitcoin. If you have a computer with a mining speed of 5 TH/s then you would get 0.033 coins in one month. In other words, it would take years for you to actually mine a bitcoin.

This timing is only going to be worse as the bitcoin moves forward. As fewer potential bitcoins are introduced, the equations that would be required for producing such coins will become even more complex. This makes it harder for you to actually get something out of a standard mining process.

Of course, you have the option to get several computers together in your property to make the mining process a little faster. But even with that, you would require more money for everything while using even more energy than what you might be comfortable with.

A larger business with many computers would have a much easier time with mining bitcoins. But even then it might take a few days for the process to work. A team would have to analyze how much it would cost to mine the coin versus the value of that coin. The prospect of mining the currency based on its potential value changes would have to be used too.

But there is a solution in that you can engage in bitcoin mining pool activities. But even with that, the total amount you would get out of it would be limited based on your effort.

How a Mining Pool Works

A bitcoin mining pool works as you use your computer's processing power to help with the mining process. You would work alongside other peoples' computers to produce equations and solutions to assist in mining a coin.

You can find many great mining pools that you can enter into. These will provide you with details on the coins that need to be mined and how you can get them ready. You would require a proper mining software program and wallet for your use.

This is a special setup but it would only pay out based on what you put in. You would be paid based on the processing power you put in and how well you can get the coins you have mined well enough.

You might not be paid too much in a pool as you would only be getting something based on what you are contributing. This is a key point for mining that must be planned ahead of time based on the computer program you plan on using.

Meanwhile, a pool fee may be charged. This would be good for 1 percent of whatever you mine in most cases. Not all pools will be this generous though. Watch for what you can get out of a mining pool so you can get into something that is appropriate and useful for your investment desires.

What About Cloud Mining?

One aspect of bitcoin mining that deserves to be discussed is cloud mining. The cloud network system that so many homes and businesses use is truly distinct and special…but does that mean cloud mining is actually useful?

With a cloud network, you can store information onto a separate server or storage spot. This works without you having to use any special software or hard disk space on your part. You just get online, log into your account and use it to your advantage.

But is cloud mining actually worthy of your time? The answer to that is simple – no.

Although cloud networking and access is convenient, this is not something that works for bitcoin mining purposes. Many groups might offer cloud mining services but there is a huge problem with that point.

Bitcoin

With cloud mining, you would be using your computer to support mining options that are run by a cloud computing site. That is, you are providing energy to a cloud server that will access something through its own program. You are not actually using your own software program in the process.

As a result, you are not necessarily working with particular mining activities in mind. You are actually causing someone else to get some kind of mining effort up and running.

This is a real problem that could keep you from getting a profit off of your mining efforts. In other words, the cloud mining activities you get into would more than likely be scams as you will not actually get what you are trying to mine.

Remember that your bitcoin mining plans will require a dedicated computer and a massive amount of effort for the process. This is ideal if you want to get your own bitcoins but be prepared to spend a lot and wait a while just to get it ready. Also, you might have to do much more than just use a single computer to actually get some kind of result off of your mining efforts.

Chapter 9:

Trading Bitcoins

As you acquire bitcoins, you can trade them in any way you see fit. While you can always spend them, you can trade them after they change in value after a while. The fact that the bitcoin changes in value quite often makes it a viable investment for your desires.

The trading plans you get into should give you many options for getting more out of the bitcoin. You can quickly move a coin around an exchange and make it work to your profit if used right.

Trade On An Exchange

The bitcoin exchange that you might have bought your bitcoins from can also be the same spot that you sell them at. You can trade your coins on that exchange and get different cryptocurrencies off of them if desired. You also have the option to get fiat currency off of your bitcoin.

Watch for any fees that come from an exchange. These should not be too large in size but do check on the rules that an exchange has posted for such coins.

Bitcoin

The types of fiat currency that you could get in such a transaction will also be limited. You might only be able to get the American dollar or euro off of your deal. Some national sites might offer more localized currency options like the British pound or Canadian dollar. Look at what you might get out of your currency before you take it out.

Also, watch for the rules relating to how much time must pass between when you buy something and when you sell it. Some exchanges might establish these rules to keep people from abusing the bitcoin system. While there are no laws stating that you must wait a certain amount of time between trades, you could still be subject to some of these rules depending on whom you are working with.

Trade Online Through a Broker

You may also consider trading your bitcoins through a broker's service. A broker will provide you with help for getting a bitcoin transaction ready. This broker can take care of the trade for you in a professional and prompt manner.

This is useful but not all brokerage firms will help you with bitcoins or other cryptocurrencies. Also, the fee might be a little higher when you work with such a person like this.

There is a chance that more groups will offer such trading services over time. Fidelity Investments has particularly been mining bitcoins and has strongly considered offering bitcoin brokerage services, for instance. Still, you should check around online to see which brokers actually offer help.

Review Trends

You have the option to analyze individual trends in the market. These include trends relating to:

- The highs and lows of the bitcoin's value
- The total volume being traded
- The supply that is available for trading purposes
- Historic information relating to how the currency has been traded in the last week, month or year

The bitcoin is treated like any other special commodity online. Use the analytical tools you can find online to figure out what trends are showing up. You might have to do your own personal analysis of the bitcoin too based on what is happening and what you might observe on the chart.

Watch the Volume

Look at the volume involved with the currency too. The volume refers to how many people are trading a currency at a certain time. The number of trades being made in a trading period is listed as the volume alongside the total value of those transactions.

The volume will impact the value of the currency in its own way. When the volume is higher, the price is more likely to make a dramatic change for the better or worse.

The changes in the bitcoin's value have especially been volatile in recent time as the volume goes up. It had a value in the three-digit range for a while but the increase in volume has caused the currency to go up to thousands of dollars in value.

What is even more interesting is that there is no real way how you can tell when the value will rise or fall. Be aware of how the volume changes and see how it influences the value of the bitcoin as you plan on trading it.

Be aware of what you could get out of your trading plans when using the bitcoin. This is an attractive thing to invest in but you should watch for how the trading process works.

Chapter 10:

How You Can Use Bitcoins

Bitcoins are great for many uses. You have already read about how you can take care of transactions with bitcoins. Whether it entails online orders or even some physical business services, you will find it easy for you to get more out of the bitcoin these days. The fact that so many places are starting to accept the bitcoin helps too.

But while you can use the bitcoin for online transactions and some in-person activities, there are many additional uses you could enjoy having when using the bitcoin. Let's take a look at some of them.

Transfer Into Fiat Money

The bitcoins you have can be transferred into fiat money. That is, the coins will be exchanged for whatever particular kind of money it is you want to utilize. This makes it easier for you to enjoy the profits off of your investment if it was successful.

You would have to transfer your bitcoin into fiat money through either a bitcoin exchange or through a bitcoin ATM. You must have information on your bitcoin wallet on hand to allow the process to go through properly.

Bitcoin

Of course, fiat money is still subject to inflation and many other problems that the bitcoin was designed to avoid. While having the added fiat money is always useful, you might consider keeping your coins for a little longer. But you have the option to do what you feel with your investment as there is no truly wrong answer for what could be done with it.

Move Money Between People

You can also move the money in your wallet between other people who have this currency on hand. The process of moving money around only takes a few moments to do and is easy provided that both people in the transaction have a wallet.

This may take a little more time to finish if you have a larger amount of money you wish to transfer. But as you move the money around, you will find how easy it is for you to get it exchanged well enough.

Don't forget that you can do this regardless of the currency the other person typically uses. The bitcoin is made to be fully universal and distinct.

Operate Online Banking Services

One great thing you can do with your bitcoins involves working with online banking functions. You can establish various great online banking processes and transactions when you work with the bitcoin.

Because the bitcoin has the same value around the world, it is easy to transfer. The online nature of the currency also allows it to stay active and useful.

Chapter 10: How You Can Use Bitcoins

More importantly, the bitcoin is useful for how it can provide people with banking services in countries or other parts of the world where traditional banking services are not available. You can get the currency to work in remote spots where it is tough to get physical money out to a spot.

For instance, the bitcoin can be found in parts of northern India where it is tough for people to reach standard banking functions. The bitcoin may work for exchanging money as it is simple and does not require any physical paper or coin materials. The money that people have can also be stored in secure wallets so the risk of fraudulent money will be eliminated.

The bitcoin would have to be introduced by outside parties and supported with a strong infrastructure that allows payments to move through well. But once everything is set up right, it becomes easier for the currency to be transferred and used up between people without problems.

Bitcoin

You will enjoy using the bitcoin for many intentions. The functionality of this currency makes it an outstanding choice for your investment needs that deserves to be noticed.

Chapter 11:

A General Look At Other Cryptocurrencies

While we have been talking about the bitcoin for a while now, it is important to note that there are many other cryptocurrencies for your use. These have been heavily inspired by the bitcoin. Of course, the blockchain arrangement of the bitcoin has allowed for the creation of other currencies.

The blockchain technology is available in the public domain. This open source setup can be altered in many ways. People have adjusted the code to the bitcoin in a few ways to create unique currencies that are different.

The main key is that even the slightest alteration in the bitcoin's code would result in the creation of a totally new currency. This is to ensure the bitcoin is separate from all the other currencies and that it stands out as a special investment choice.

This look at cryptocurrencies is an extremely brief analysis of the many different currencies you can find today. There are far too many of these currencies to talk about right now, what with the field developing so well.

Ethereum

The Ethereum coin is a popular option for investing that is second behind the bitcoin in terms of its popularity. This is a coin that is relatively similar to the bitcoin but actually has an infinite amount of coins that you could mine.

It uses a longer key series for individual coins. That is, the names and identifying points on coins could be very long simply to support how the coin can be produced as often as desired. Like the bitcoin, the mining process takes longer when more coins have already been made. But miners have no limits for how many coins they can produce, thus allowing them to keep running their campaigns for as long as desired.

Ethereum uses smart contracts in each transaction. This works in that the information on one's assets will be shared in real time through a network. The proof of membership and any virtual assets the owner has will be highlighted on each Ethereum coin that you have. This provides you with the opportunity to keep what you have accessible and ready for use.

Litecoin

Another coin to look into is the Litecoin. This is a special type of coin that uses a code system that helps you to produce the coin in as little time as possible.

The coding terms on the Litecoin are smaller as there are fewer characters and equations needed to produce a coin. Each coin is still worth less than what you would get out of most other cryptocurrencies.

Chapter 11: A General Look At Other Cryptocurrencies

The Litecoin is an interesting option for investing for how it can be produced fast and does not require an extensive timeframe for mining. But the smaller code used means that it could be easier for people to duplicate. Be aware of this when investing as you do not want to fall into some scheme that might not be fully legitimate.

Zcash

Another popular cryptocurrency to find is Zcash. It is an investment option that is noteworthy for being fully anonymous. It does not record address information whether it entails a wallet or an IP address. It never asks for anyone's personal data either. This allows for transactions with the Zcash currency to move through efficiently and without outside data getting in the way of things.

This special currency is also noted for using fewer algorithms in the mining and transaction process. It moves through quickly and only takes a short bit of time to mine when compared with the bitcoin.

Still, the Zcash currency is not in circulation as well as the bitcoin is. Not everyone is taking it in either. In addition, the Zcash option is cheaper in value than what you would find elsewhere. The value does not change too often either; this could offer a sense of consistency but it is not necessarily going to be a prominent long term investment choice.

Zcash does not have much of a trading volume as many other currencies either. This allows for the value of the currency to be under a little more control than what people might find elsewhere.

Specialized Options

Some cryptocurrencies are made with very specific demands in mind. These are specialized currencies that are organized with limited activities. These cater to people who are more interested in those certain actions.

These particular currencies work in that they target people who use certain websites or services. People can acquire such coins and use them to pay for items relating to particular fields.

The FirstBlood and NeverDie currencies are two options to note here. These focus on esports games. Such games are ones that entail people going online and competing against each other. The League of Legends game is one particular example of an esports game.

By using FirstBlood and NeverDie coins, a player can acquire skins and other items for use in esports games. They can also use these coins to bet on professional esports activities.

Another example is the NoLimitCoin. This currency was developed in the middle part of 2017 as one for fantasy sports use. People who use this coin can spend it on covering their entry fees into online fantasy sports activities. They can compete in those sports leagues to win prizes like more of these coins that can be traded out as fiat currency later.

This example is interesting in that it could provide people with a way to make big money. If the NoLimitCoin increases in value then that means a person could withdraw one's winnings with a significant profit involving not only winning more coins but also from the value of the coin increasing.

Chapter 11: A General Look At Other Cryptocurrencies

There are no rules as to what specific cryptocurrencies could be utilized for. The fragmentation of the industry only shows just how viable and distinct the field is.

More Will Come Later

Be on the lookout for other cryptocurrencies as time goes along. The great thing about these currencies is that they can be prepared in many forms based on how the code to the blockchain system is changed around. There is no way how anyone can tell where the cryptocurrency field will go next.

Of course, the bitcoin is still going to be the golden standard to watch for when it comes to noticing how the cryptocurrency field is evolving. The bitcoin is popular for how it is a stronger investment option that has a sturdy base to it.

Chapter 12:

The Future of the Bitcoin

Everything you have been reading here with regards to the bitcoin shows that it is indeed a currency that deserves to be noticed. This special currency is powerful and popular for being an investment option that could go places. Its increased functionality and the public's ongoing acceptance of it make this a useful currency to have too.

But there are many things to watch for with regards to where the bitcoin will go. There is no telling what the future of the bitcoin truly holds. But we can at least surmise a few points out of it.

More Countries Start to Use the Bitcoin

The bitcoin has been accepted in many parts of the world. That total number of parts is only going to increase as time goes along. As people start to see how well the bitcoin can be used, they will begin to take it in for many intentions.

The growth of the bitcoin is clearly noticeable. In early 2017, Japan started to accept the bitcoin as legal tender for many government-based transactions. While the bitcoin had been prominent in that country for a while, this expansion in how it can be used is significant as it increases how people can use the currency.

Countries like China that have been sour on the bitcoin could always change their minds on how the currency can be used too. Keep an eye out for the latest news on the bitcoin to see what could happen.

On a related note, it should become easier for bitcoins to be traded in more markets. As word on the bitcoin gets out there, people all around the world will want to buy and sell their bitcoins on the market. This should add to how active the bitcoin trading market is. It does make the coin a little more volatile though.

Brokerage Support

The fact that Fidelity Investments has been working on mining bitcoins in recent time is proof that brokers of all sorts may start to work with bitcoins in the future. Any broker that works with bitcoins would have a new avenue with which to market one's services and efforts.

This is a special point but a broker who wants to offer bitcoin support must be analyzed carefully. A broker will certainly charge more for one's services because of the professional nature of the transaction. The belief that the broker might know more about the coin could also be a big point to see.

As for the mining processes, there is always the chance that bitcoins and other cryptocurrencies may be included in funds. The use of mutual funds has been popular for many retirement savings needs. Just think, you could contact a broker in the future to learn about the bitcoin and to get into a fund that is based off of the bitcoin's performance.

More Retailers Start to Use Bitcoins

As you read earlier, the bitcoin has been accepted by many online and physical retailers around the world. The odds of the total number of groups accepting it increasing are expected to be rather strong. This comes as people start to see how well the bitcoin can be used for their investment needs and how the currency can work.

Appropriate software is still needed for allowing the currency to work. The proper wallet program and software to read and process transactions are required. Fortunately, the free market for the bitcoin ensures that people can download programs for bitcoin use that are totally free to use. This should only make it easier for businesses to want to use the bitcoin for their intentions.

Do watch for how retailers start to use the bitcoin. You are more likely to see smaller businesses start to use the bitcoin because it might be easier for those people to start bitcoin-related operations without too many payment processing portals involved. But when more large retailers start accepting it, you will notice that this is indeed something worth exploring for how prominent and thrilling of an investment it truly is.

More Miners

It is going to take a while for the bitcoin to reach its limit of 21 million coins to be mined. The process of producing coins should be a little faster though as more miners get in on the bitcoin game.

As more countries review the bitcoin, miners from those countries will start to engage in their own activities. South

Bitcoin

Korea is a good example of this, for instance. More than 10 percent of all bitcoin trades in the world happen in South Korea. This comes as regulations on the bitcoin have expanded in early 2017. This in turn allowed more people to see what the bitcoin is like while also producing more mining teams in Korea.

Those new miners will not be limited to just one or two countries. They will come from any spot where mining activities can be held in.

Watch For More Competitors...and a Lack of Knowledge

There will be many other competitors out there who will try and release their own cryptocurrencies to contend with the bitcoin. There are more than a thousand known cryptocurrencies out there already.

In fact, if you look at an ICO website then you will see just how the alternatives are growing. These ICOs, or Initial Coin Offerings, are events where people can purchase new currency coins from brand new cryptocurrencies being formed. Such ICOs are being promoted with unique features in each coin or specific standards for how the blockchain technology will be used.

A majority of these ICOs are not necessarily trying to go head on against the bitcoin though. They are mostly investment opportunities used to raise funds for extensive projects that an operator wants to tackle in the future. These provide promises of profits as the values of these coins go up although they are still risky endeavors. There are no guarantees that their value will actually rise.

Chapter 12: The Future of the Bitcoin

Naturally, some of those competitors might be questionable in nature. These include groups that do not fully understand the intricacies of how the bitcoin works.

One example of this could come from celebrities starting up their own ICOs. They might start these up with the intention of raising funds for certain projects but in many cases they might just use their star power to make their ICOs more attractive. They might not have a clear understanding of how well an ICO is organized and how it works.

The lack of knowledge of how cryptocurrencies work could be the death of many great endeavors. People will need to learn more about the bitcoin and the currency concept in general if they are to actually enjoy using it. Remember, cryptocurrency is not a get rich quick kind of affair.

What About a Physical Currency Format?

Finally, it is important to note that physical options for using the bitcoin will expand over time. Expect to see more cards that can link up to bitcoin wallets on the market in the future. These would use specific chip features that contain the information relating to your wallet on it.

As you read earlier, a bitcoin card could work like any credit card except that it goes on your bitcoin wallet. It would only work in spots that do accept the bitcoin though.

Do not expect to see physical coins with the bitcoin logo on them though. Those images you see of physical bitcoins are just illustrative. They symbolize how the bitcoin could be worth a grand amount of money and as simply for show purposes.

Bitcoin

Expect the bitcoin to keep growing in popularity. Whether the actual value of the currency will grow is unclear but it is something to note. After all, people are always interested in seeing how the financial world will evolve.

Conclusion

As you have read throughout this guide, the bitcoin is a type of investment option that is truly something to explore. The bitcoin has an outstanding layout for it that gives you the opportunity to earn a large amount of money if you are smart in your investment plans.

The bitcoin has been growing as it is being accepted in more places and is supporting by an ever-growing community of users and enthusiasts. But as you see how the bitcoin grows and evolves, you should also look at how it works.

We hope this guide has helped you to understand everything about the bitcoin and how you can use it. As you utilize the points in this guide, be certain you look at how you are acquiring your coins and how you will use them. Check on what services are available for you and test out different programs as you wish.

Do be advised though that the bitcoin, like with any other investment, can be a risky endeavor. You must do your research and analysis carefully before you use or invest in the bitcoin. This is needed to help you figure out what you could be doing with the coin.

Make sure you also understand how the bitcoin works and that you know what can influence its value and functionality. It is a

Bitcoin

highly viable investment but it could also be troublesome if you are not careful enough with it.

Enjoy your adventures with the bitcoin. You will enjoy every step of the ride as you use the right ideas and strategies for utilizing it to your advantage. You might be surprised at what you will get out of your experience with the bitcoin whether you plan on using it or saving it up as a long term investment.

Made in the USA
Lexington, KY
21 December 2017